The

EXPERT'S GUIDE
to

POSITIVE
CONFLICT

Dr. Stephen L. Kalaluhi

ISBN-13: 978-1523720576

ISBN-10: 1523720573

To my wife Gina…

my inspiration, my motivation,

my drive to succeed.

"Many women do noble things, but you surpass them all."

Proverbs 31:29

TABLE OF CONTENTS

INTRODUCTION:

INTRODUCTION

The Cost of Conflict

"I am not afraid of an army of lions led by a sheep;

I am afraid of an army of sheep led by a lion."

- Alexander the Great

In 2008, the publishers of the Myers-Brigg Assessment and the Thomas-Kilmann Conflict Mode Instrument conducted a study designed to understand the cost of conflict within organizations. What their research uncovered was almost unbelievable: 85% of those who participated in the research stated that they dealt with workplace conflict on a frequent or regular basis; employees spent 2.8 hours each week dealing with the negative effects and fall-out of conflict; 27% of participants were personally insulted or verbally attacked while at work; 25% of participants burned a sick day because they didn't want to deal with conflict in the office; 9% of those in the study blamed conflict for failed projects and initiatives; and most eye-opening, conflict costed organizations more than $350 billion in lost productivity and opportunities for growth.

Armed with this knowledge, the most important question to answer becomes, "How do I resolve conflict within my organization in such a way that not only addresses the negative effects of conflict, but turns it into a positive and productive outcome that results in growth and opportunities to succeed?" Answering this one question is what this Expert's Guide is all about – equipping you and your organization to turn the negative effects of conflict into positive outcomes and opportunities for growth.

The Expert's Guide to Positive Conflict provides you with a proven methodology for resolving conflict that is highly effective, yet elegantly simple, and built upon an eight step process that includes opening a dialogue between all parties involved, getting those involved to focus on the process instead of on the people, creating an environment where listening to differing viewpoints is not only encouraged but expected, identifying common ground between those affected, determining those things that need to be addressed first, creating an actionable plan that all parties agree to, committing to following through and executing on the plan, and agreeing to celebrating wins as they occur. These eight keys align your team when conflict arises and gives you the framework needed to allow conflict to result in the growth and development within your organization.

No one enjoys having to deal with conflict, and the negative consequences associated with conflict are evidenced in the research completed in 2008. What's important to remember, however, is that while no one invites conflict into their organizations, the fact that conflict exists should be seen as an opportunity for growth as opposed to something that can derail momentum and success. This mindset shift occurs as the result of recognizing that conflict typically occurs when people who care about what they're doing stand up for what they believe is right, especially when they don't agree with the how what they believe in is being handled. Your challenge is to capitalize on that passion, turning it into an opportunity to strengthen your organization while solidifying trust in, and commitment to, each other.

KEY #1:

Open a Dialogue

"To effectively communicate, we must realize that we are all different in the way we perceive the world and use this understanding as a guide to our communication with others."

- Tony Robbins

The first key to resolving conflict requires you to make space for dialogue. In fact, one of the first things to deteriorate when conflict occurs is communication. What's interesting to note, however, is that the large majority of conflict can be traced back to ineffective communication. The secret to effective communication can be found in the opening sentence of this chapter: you must make space for it to occur. Making space for communication to occur is the key because it forces you to set aside time to purposefully get everyone involved in the conflict into the same place, at the same time, with the intent of creating a safe environment for everyone to speak their minds.

A Safe Environment

The natural tendency of those involved in conflict is to shut down, to not want to talk about it, to ignore it in the hopes that it will go away on its own. As a leader, you must be courageous enough to do what it takes to address the situation, no matter how uncomfortable, or how awkward it might be. Your role as a leader is to facilitate the discussion in such a way that everyone involved has the freedom to openly speak their mind, openly communicate their point of view, and openly discuss why they believe what they believe.

Set the Ground Rules

Getting those involved in conflict into the same room at the same time is sometimes a victory in and of itself. The last thing you want to do is waste the opportunity you're presented with. One way to ensure you make the most of the opportunity is to set, and agree to, rules of engagement as it relates to everyone speaking their mind. Only want one person to speak at a time? Make it a rule of that meeting. Don't want anyone interrupting when someone else is sharing? Make that a rule, too. What about non-verbal communications? Your rules should absolutely cover body language, because what isn't said out loud is sometimes louder, and more painful, than what is said out loud. Once you've gone through the rules of engagement for your meeting, ensure all parties involved agree to the terms as you've explained them. Let them know that their verbal agreement is a binding and critical component to the success of the meeting, as well as to resolving the conflict.

Agree to the Goal

Now that you have verbal agreement regarding what you expect in regards to participant behavior, the next step to opening dialogue is agreeing on the desired outcome. You're not there to listen to your team complain or air its dirty laundry. You are there to resolve the conflict that is preventing your organization from flourishing and thriving. What's your desired outcome, and does it align with what your team is expecting? The only way to know for sure is to ask. The process of clarifying expectations and outcomes ensures that you stay focused if emotions run rampant, and clarifying expectations and outcomes ensures that those involved know exactly what you expect from them, and what they can expect from each other.

Now Let's Talk

Frustration occurs when those on your team don't feel like what they say matters. Conflict occurs when those in your organization don't feel like their voice is valued. You are responsible for making sure everyone present believes they have the opportunity to speak openly and freely about whatever it is that is causing the conflict. They must be given every chance to share what they need to share, and be given every chance to say what they need to say. It is at this point that you will need to stand your ground, and it is at this point that you will need to enforce the rules you agreed to earlier. This emotionally charged meeting will quickly deteriorate if you don't take a stand and create the space your people need to feel comfortable enough to get off their chest what needs to be shared.

Establish early on that what you say, goes. Remind those participating that your overarching goal is to resolve the conflict at hand so that you can get back to the business of growing your team. You don't have the time or the luxury to wait around for conflict to resolve itself on its own, so your entire purpose is focused on getting your team back on track and playing for the same team again.

Positive Conflict Starts Here

Opening dialogue between those involved in the conflict only adds value if those involved trust you and trust that the environment is safe enough to share. This first key to resolving conflict within your organization requires you to do whatever you need to do to make sure people start talking. Talking leads to dialogue, and dialogue is the first step to resolving conflict. Transforming the negative effects of conflict revolves around teaching your people how to communicate. Once they understand the value of dialogue and learn the process of resolving that conflict through positive dialogue, they will be able to work through any future challenges they face. The more you emphasize the importance of dialoguing, the more your people will come to see how it correlates to building a successful and thriving organizational culture. The stronger your organizational culture becomes, the easier it will be for dialogue to occur. This is one cycle you definitely want your team on.

KEY #2:

Process, Not Person

"Conflict cannot survive without participation."

- Wayne Dyer

Now that a dialogue has been opened and you've successfully completed the first step in resolving conflict, the next step is to keep the focus on the process in question, instead of allowing it to become about any one person. This is an important aspect of the process for you to facilitate, because as a leader your primary concern needs to be solidifying the process, while

13

simultaneously bringing your team to a place where they respect and trust each other enough to hear differing points of view and alternative suggestions as to how the process can be made better.

When the focus of a conflict within your organization shifts from being about a person to being about what's best for the organization, those involved are more apt to hear what others have to say. When it's not about any one person, then all the history and drama is removed and both sides are more able to see what is most beneficial to the organization, as well as what is in the best interest of your team. Focusing those in conflict on the process allows for decisions to be made that are free from negative emotions, past hurts, or preconceived notions that are typically associated with a person.

Your role in this process is to constantly and continuously keep the focal point of the discussion centered on the process. This can be accomplished by watching out for the language used when in dialogue, as well as by keeping the words used as positive as possible. While in the dialogue phase, those participants may choose to voice their hurts and why they feel slighted by the other party. Don't shy away from this or try to shut it down, as it is a crucial part of the healing process. The dialogue is an opportunity for participants to get things off their chest that they probably bottled up because they never thought they'd get the chance to share. Allowing your team to vent is an important part of this process, but it is critical that as you challenge those involved to keep the language used self-focused, rather than judgmental and blaming, positive and forward-leaning, rather than negative and stuck in the past.

Watch for Language

If participants choose to share, ensure that the language used is conducive to growing through this process. Keeping the dialogue self-focused is a great way to ensure this occurs. For example, saying, "I feel disrespected and of less value to the organization when you speak to me the way you do," is a more productive statement than, "You're a disrespectful oaf who doesn't value anyone's opinion other than your own." The value in this approach is two-fold: First, you can't argue with what a person is feeling. Their perceptions are their own, but more importantly, their perceptions are their reality. Second, this approach helps keep the defenses lowered. If you come at me telling me I don't do this right or that I'm wrong with that, my initial reaction is going to be to protect myself. When this happens, the chances of success diminish greatly.

Building a culture where your people focus on those things that they can control (e.g. how they feel, or what they perceive to be true, etc.) is paramount to resolving conflict and building a healthy organization. Those who point blame at others for how they feel take on a victim mindset that prevents them from seeing how their own actions perpetuate and escalate the conflict. Those who focus on themselves, however, take responsibility for their own thoughts, for their own actions (and reactions), and for their own outcomes. When your people take responsibility for their role in a conflict, the conflict becomes much easier to resolve and grow through.

Keep It Positive

Keeping the communication and dialogue focused on the process instead of on the person is a much simpler task to accomplish when the words used are positive and encouraging. It's important to recognize that those coming to this dialogue have been hurt and feel as though they've been wronged in some way or another. Keeping the focus on the process is easier when positive words and phrases are associated with accomplishing a shared goal or common vision.

One way to keep this process moving in the right direction is to keep the discussion forward-focused. It's too easy to fall into what happened in the past, and it's too easy to get historical when it comes to hurts and offenses. When you keep the verbiage allowed positive and focused on what you can accomplish together, you're able to paint a picture of what the process could, and should, look like when your team or organization is firing on all cylinders.

Positive Conflict Starts Here

This key is perhaps the most beneficial to turning conflict into positive gains within your organization. When your team gets to the point where they can openly disagree about the process, instead of focusing on the person who brought it up, true transformation becomes possible. Making conflict about the process focuses the attention on how you and your organization can be better, rather than focusing on past hurts and negative perceptions.

At the end of the day, your organization is only as strong as the structure, process, and systems you use to keep it running smoothly and efficiently. Focusing on making the structure, process, and systems better is a crucial aspect of continuous growth and purposeful development. Conflict arises when people take suggestions personally, so bringing your people back to the importance of making the process better allows for disagreements to turn into opportunities for improvement.

KEY #3:

Actively Listen

"A man who has no imagination has no wings."

- Muhammad Ali

    The first key to resolving conflict revolved around giving people an opportunity to share what was on their heart. The second key to resolving conflict encouraged you to keep the process at the center of discussion instead of it being about a person. The third key to resolving conflict deals with keeping the listening active. Active listening is exactly what it sounds like, and requires effort, energy, and participation from all involved. Transformation will not occur if one side of the conflict mentally checks out while the other side is sharing their hurts and sharing their perceptions.

Active Listening Takes Effort

Active listening requires participants to remain present, to not day-dream, to stay focused on what the other person is saying. It's important to recognize that active listening is not a skill that comes naturally to most people. In fact, most people don't really listen for the sake of listening, they listen so they can recognize when it's their turn to speak next. Here are a few tips to help you ensure participants actively listen:

Ask for Clarification

Ask the listening party what they heard. Start them with the following prompt: "I heard you say…," then have them finish the statement with the following prompt: "Did I understand you correctly, or is there anything you would like to add further clarification to?" Clarifying statements is a great exercise you can use to ensure what is being said is the same as what is being heard.

The value of active listening is found in repeating what the listener heard in order to verify and confirm comprehension occurred. Communication often times breaks down when a person says one thing, but the listener hears something totally different. You're not asking for the listener to repeat verbatim what was stated, but rather you are asking them to paraphrase and restate what they heard. When an individual paraphrases and restates what they heard, the likelihood of internalizing what they heard becomes much greater. Internalizing dialogue takes comprehension one step further because it becomes more about how what was said affects me, rather than just how what was said affects the other person.

Ask Probing Questions

As you facilitate this process, don't allow participants to stay skin deep. Conflict resolution requires those involved to go much deeper than merely staying on the surface. Throughout the discussion, interject probing questions when you feel those sharing are holding back, or are fearful of fully sharing. "How did that make you feel," or "Why did you respond in the way you did," or "How would you have preferred this situation be handled" are all great examples of probing questions designed to go deeper and create a better understanding of the underlying root cause of the conflict itself. One thing to note: when asking probing questions, be prepared for the answers you receive. I've worked with individuals in the past that broke into tears after a probing question because her reaction to a situation was rooted in how she was treated by her father growing up. While you're not a counselor, it is important to remember that we all bring our humanity to the table.

Don't Let It Go

Don't move on in the discussion if the listening party isn't fully comprehending what is being said. Active listening is about participating in the discussion for the purpose of fully understanding what is being said. If those involved don't fully get what is being shared, don't ignore it and move on. Challenge those involved to stay fully engaged. Continue to ask clarifying and probing questions until what is being said is crystal clear.

There is a direct correlation between active listening and productivity within your organization. One of the beneficial side effects of improving active listening is that you team becomes better equipped to negotiate with one another when disagreements do arise. Their ability to really hear what the other person has to say, then internalize by paraphrasing and restating it, gives your team the skills they need to come to agreements on issues and initiatives where there might not be any common ground. When no common ground is found between parties, moving forward with the idea that makes the most sense becomes easier as the result of actively listening, and participating in the process of hearing all sides of the issue.

Positive Conflict Starts Here

Active listening is a skill set that is not only valuable in resolving conflict, but is valuable throughout every aspect of your organization. Teaching your team to actively listen ensures that conflict in the future results in growth by not allowing miscommunications to escalate. When your people truly feel like they've been heard, it's easier to move on and make the changes that need to be made. One of the natural byproducts of active listening is the improved ability to persuade others. Active listening gives those with the best ideas and most merit a bigger voice at the table, while still allowing for all parties involved the opportunity to state their case. Actively participating in this manner renders the conflict less about the person and more about the process.

KEY #4:

Agree to Disagree

"Success is never final. Failure is never fatal. It is courage that counts."

- Winston Churchill

As you facilitate the process of resolving conflict, stay cognizant of those points that your people agree on and those points they disagree on. The fourth key in this process requires you to take inventory of the common ground your team shares, as well as take stock of those issues they still don't see eye-to-eye on yet. Your goal is to dig deep enough to understand where the gap is in those things they still disagree on, while at the same time keeping those things they agree on in the forefront of their minds. Reminding them of what it feels like and what it looks like to agree on an issue is a great way to grease the wheels of team unity.

It Takes Courage

Don't shy away from the issues that are still cause for concern. Lesser leaders rest on their laurels when they get to this point and are happy with the fact that their team agrees on anything at all. Don't fall into this trap, because any issue left undiscussed and unresolved has the potential to spark into yet another flame. From a process standpoint, start by stating an issue that both parties agreed to, then ask both sides to discuss how they were able to arrive at a mutually beneficial middle ground. After both sides share, immediately bring to the table an issue they haven't agreed on yet, and ask them to utilize the same process with this issue that they used with the issue they were able to agree on.

Stand your ground once again, and don't back down. Don't let those involved believe that resolution can't be found. Continue to refer back to how they came to an agreement on the previous issue, then challenge them to follow the same pattern one disagreed upon issue at a time. Of all the keys to resolving conflict, this one represents the greatest amount of challenge to you as a facilitator, and represents the greatest amount of effort needed on your part to do well.

Negotiate Well

Those issues that are left unresolved require you to maneuver and negotiate on behalf of both sides in order to achieve your desired outcome. Negotiations start with both sides agreeing to a mutually beneficial outcome. Once both sides agree to the outcome, it becomes a game of who is going to break first in order to get what they want. By keeping their eyes on the prize, you can ensure this does not become the case. In any negotiation, compromise must be made on both sides Both sides must make certain concessions that they feel are of equal value if the negotiations are to be successful. Your role in this matter is to ensure that both sides are treated equally well, and that what is conceded in the process of negotiating is of equal value.

If All Else Fails

What happens if you find that both sides reach an impasse and can't agree to a mutually beneficial path forward? Unfortunately, this is a very real possibility, but it doesn't signify the end of the line in regards to resolving conflict. When an impasse is reached, it is crucial that you have both sides agree to the fact that they are at an impasse and acknowledge the challenges they face in resolving that particular issue, and agree to a date and time where they can reengage in working toward finding a mutually beneficial solution.

Make Progress Visible

It's easy to sweep issues under the rug when they aren't front of mind. As you move on from this step, it is important that you communicate the wins, as well as communicate the issues that still need work. Making the positive results public serves as a great example to the organization of what is possible when conflict is resolved, and making the unresolved issues public creates an informal accountability system regarding what still requires action from those involved. Discretion is important, but generalizing your victories and your unresolved challenges is enough to keep people focused on making the organization a better place to work, improving the systems that govern organizational actions, and strengthening the overall culture of your organization.

Positive Conflict Starts Here

The greatest aspect of this key is found in the reference to those issues that both parties found agreement in. Remembering the victories and successes, no matter how small or insignificant they might seem, is a great way to keep your organization focused on the positive. It is naïve to believe that building a flourishing and thriving organization is going to be unicorns and rainbows all the time, so you need a strategy in place to deal with the challenges and obstacles your organization is sure to face. Helping your people remember their past victories is a great way to keep momentum moving forward.

Sometimes agreeing to disagree is all it takes to open the doors of dialogue and negotiations. Your job is to make people aware of those things they hold in common, no matter how ridiculous you think the commonalities are. Remember, your goal in all of this is to strengthen your organization to the point where they can resolve conflict on their own, and in such a way that leaves you free to focus on the strategies needed to help your organization secure it's foothold in your marketplace.

KEY #5:

Prioritize the Conflicts

"You must speak to the soul in order to electrify the man."

- Napoleon Bonaparte

Healing past hurts takes time. Don't walk into this process thinking you're going to walk out of the meeting with everyone hugging and hanging out after their shifts end. Yes, this is a start. But that is all it is. The next key in this process focuses on developing a list of priorities to address in regards to getting your team back on track. The sooner your team gets back on track, the sooner you and the rest of your organization can focus on building a flourishing and thriving organization.

Ride the Wave

You created momentum with the last key to resolving conflict, and this key to conflict resolution feeds off that momentum by getting both sides to agree on creating a priority list of those things that must be addressed in order to achieve continued success. On a white board or large piece of paper, list out every issue you uncovered throughout this process. Under each issue listed, determine how conflict in that area negatively impacted your team or organization, then list out what your team would look like if you could snap your fingers and make it all better.

Pick One Thing

Prioritizing your list may prove as challenging as negotiating from the last step, but the step is not without its merit. You could easily tell those in the meeting that you're going to decide how the priority list is going to work, but you would be overlooking another opportunity to solidify the trust and rapport building between both affected sides. One method to get two sides to agree on priorities is called the "pick one" method. The beauty of this method is that it unifies the group to look at the benefits of completing a task, rather than focusing on their own personal gain or benefit.

The way the method works is you start with all the priorities listed on a whiteboard or large sheet of paper. Then you ask those in participation to identify which task they would choose to complete if they were only allowed the time and resources to complete one task. Challenge each side to communicate why they chose the task they chose, and challenge each side to employ their active listening skills to ensure they fully comprehended and understood what it was that was said and communicated.

Repeat this process with both sides, even if they select the same task. You want to ensure the reasons for their selection are communicated because those reasons are associated with specific expectations. Take your team through the process of negotiating and making concessions where needed if they don't initially agree on a task to complete. If you must, add values to each task in the case you need to be the tie-breaker. Speaking in terms of return on investment helps those involved see how their actions affect the bottom line of the organization. Once a task is selected and agreed upon, remove it from the list, then repeat this process with the remaining tasks on the list.

A Common Goal

The beauty of creating a shared priority list with tasks to accomplish is the fact that you automatically build into this process a shared vision around a common goal. When both sides agree to a singular task to complete, they put into place those organizational components needed to improve trust, as well as those organizational components needed to become a high performing team. Having a common goal is the precursor to building and strengthening the culture of your organization, and is effective in uniting a group of individuals toward a shared vision of what the organization could, and should, look like.

This common goal also works to keep those involved from allowing their differences from derailing any momentum achieved throughout this process. The accountability created by driving toward a common goal is sometimes all that's needed to get your organization back on the right path. Let's face it, no one wants to be reason an initiative or project fails, so utilize the positive peer pressure that having an agreed upon common goal creates.

Positive Conflict Starts Here

Empowering those within your team or organization to prioritize task lists is beneficial to any and all projects related to the growth and development of your company. Giving your team the tools they need to come to agreements regarding those initiatives that will add the most value to your organization is the first step in creating and building a culture of continuous growth and improvement. What's most valuable to your organization is the positive peer pressure that is created after a task is agreed to. Continue to work with each side to ensure they don't fall back into any bad habits, and openly and publicly praise them from achieving or completing each task. Being able to communicate and associate the value of each task to the organization's bottom line is a great motivator for finishing agreed upon tasks. This also helps those within your organization to better understand how their actions positively or negatively affect the overall success of the organization.

Most individuals caught in the middle of conflict find it extremely difficult to see how their actions and behaviors negatively affect anything outside their immediate sphere of influence. Adding value to those items completed on the task list shifts mindsets from an individual viewpoint to a corporate one. When this shift occurs, conflict shifts from the individual perspective to a corporate one, as well. This shift gives your entire organization eyes to see how the overall health of the company ebbs and flows based upon the immediate thoughts and actions of its people.

KEY #6:

Create a Plan

"Every champion started off as a contender who

refused to give up."

- Rocky Balboa

Agreeing to a list of priorities is great in that it creates a shared vision and common goal, but a shared task without a plan is nothing but a wish. The sixth key to resolving conflict revolves

45

around ensuring all parties understand how the conflict is going to be resolved. You and your team may have a firm grasp on why it's important to resolve this conflict, and you may even know what all is involved. The most important question that you need to answer, however, isn't "why" or "what" but rather, "how." This key speaks to the "how" of your priority list of actions.

How Will You Do It?

Building on the momentum gained from successfully completing and implementing the last five keys to positive conflict, the next step is to ensure everyone involved understands how you're going to get to where you envision your organization being. At this point in the process, it should be clear that conflict has no place in your organization if your desire includes growth or increase. What your team might struggle with, however, is being able to see how they are going to get from where they're currently at, to where you need them to be.

As a leader, this is one of the most critical components to successfully turning conflict into positive growth and development. Not only is it important for you and your team to understand how this process is going to result in the attainment of a stronger culture, they need to believe that they can actually accomplish the plan you've laid out before them. Here's the thing: the best plans in the world will fail if those executing the plan don't see in their heads how it can be accomplished.

Be Specific

Take your list of priorities, and one by one, create a vision of what your team or organization will look like once that task is completed. Then challenge those involved to communicate with each other how that vision will be achieved. This is one step where the more detailed you are, the easier it becomes to see how the task can be accomplished. Here are a few questions that should be answered for each task identified by those in conflict:

- By when will the task be completed?
- How will we know when the task is completed?
- What measurements will we use to ensure we stay on track?
- What am I responsible for in completing this task?
- What are you responsible for in completing this task?
- What joint accountabilities do we share in completing this task?
- How much time will you commit daily, weekly, and monthly to completing this task?
- To whom can we turn if we need additional support?
- How will we celebrate when this task is satisfactorily completed?

You should add your own questions to this list, as the more detail you cover in this section, the easier it becomes for those involved to see the task as something they can accomplish together.

Push Back When Needed

It's up to you to offer feedback throughout this process that speaks to the need for a better understanding of how the process is going to work. This is not the place for ambiguity, or grey zones, or assumptions. This is your opportunity to tap into the collective to ensure those involved have zero questions about what step is next, how that steps adds value to your organization, or why that step is crucial to the overall success of your team.

With that said, it's up to you to ask the questions that need to be asked. Don't settle for answers that aren't crystal clear. Don't allow your people to get away with unknowns. Stop your team from being comfortable in the grey zone.

Continue to push back until your team gets to the point where they are arguing with you regarding the validity of how they are going to accomplish each task. Once you bring your team to a place where they are adamantly standing up for their plan, you've won.

Positive Conflict Starts Here

Like every other key to resolving conflict within your organization discussed thus far, this one too has the potential to positively affect your entire organization. Challenging your organization with gaining super clarity on how a task is going to be accomplished takes your teams' head out of the clouds and focuses them on the realities of working in the real world. Motivating and inspiring your organization is something you should absolutely do (and frequently), but that motivation and inspiration must be tethered to plans of action that actually have the teeth needed to gain the traction and momentum needed to become a sustainable and scalable process within your company. The key here is creating an exciting vision that is backed by an achievable "how."

KEY #7:

Execute the Plan

"Strength does not come from winning. Your struggles develop your strengths."

- Arnold Schwarzenegger

Now that you have successfully agreed to how the conflict will be resolved and have no questions as to who is responsible for what, or when the task will be completed by, or what the accountabilities are for both sides, you can now move forward into the doing it phase. This key focuses on action. This is where the rubber hits the proverbial road.

Get It Done

Everything you've done to this point has been in preparation for putting the process, steps, and belief system into place so that pulling the trigger and executing on the plan is seamless and painless. With the focus now on doing, it is essential that you build into the process milestones and progress markers designed to give you an overall sense of how each task is going. This part of the process may occur over the course of weeks, months, or even years, so it is important that you regularly meet with those involved to ensure momentum isn't lost and that focus is maintained.

Pleasure Based Rewards

I recognize that accomplishing and completing each task on your priority list is in addition to your teams' daily roles and responsibilities. I also recognize that this task list might end up taking a back seat when it comes to completing those daily functions required of your people and their roles within the organization. While resolving conflict and experiencing the positive benefits associated with a stronger and more resilient organizational culture should be reward enough, sometimes those involved need a little more motivation and inspiration to continuously perform tasks that are above and beyond their normal scope of duties.

What positive rewards are you authorized to award those involved in the conflict to motivate them to staying focused on completing each task on the priority list? Monetary bonuses? A day off from work? Public recognition or accolades? More importantly, what would those involved prefer as a reward for doing what you've asked them to do?

Pain Based Consequences

If the rewards for accomplishing tasks directly related to resolving conflict within your organization doesn't sit well with you, then what pain based consequences are you authorized to place on the table if those involved don't accomplish each task on your priority list? Can you dock their pay? Pull them from choice projects? Terminate their employment?

Clearly Communicate What Happens If...

Regardless of whether you reward your team for going above and beyond, or punish them for not performing at the levels you expected from them, you must clearly communicate what will happen if they do or don't complete a task. Your expectations do no one any good if you keep them to yourself. At the end of the day, you want to set up your team to succeed, and making sure they completely understand the rules of engagement is a critical component as it pertains to you achieving a desired outcome.

Positive Conflict Starts Here

Getting things done is what you are in place to do. As a leader, your role is to equip your organization to do what needs to get done in order to grow, flourish, and thrive. The process of executing a plan escapes more leaders than will admit, but the fact that this key is one of the last keys in the process of resolving conflict should speak to just how much preparation is needed in order to successfully implement an initiative or organizational shift. Skipping the keys before this one will create confusion, build resentment towards your leadership, and result in a frustrated team of individuals unsure of how their efforts will achieve the organization's desired results. Showing your organization how involved the planning process truly is will equip your people to apply the mindset of proper planning to every project and initiative you work towards achieving.

KEY #8:

Celebrate

"Notice that the stiffest tree is most easily cracked,

while the bamboo and willow survives by bending

with the wind."

- Bruce Lee

A lot of blood, sweat, and tears went into getting you and your team to this place. It's not uncommon for conflict within the workplace to have a deep structure of roots dug deep into years of strife and turmoil, so it becomes imperative that you celebrate any and all victories. This final key to resolving conflict within the workplace serves as a reminder of the importance of the celebration, what it signifies, and what it means to your organization.

Hip, Hip, Hooray!

This the last key to resolving conflict within your organization, but unfortunately, this key more often times than not gets overlooked as being unimportant to the successful completion of those tasks on your priority list. This could not be further from the truth, and the importance of celebrating your victories cannot be overstated. Those involved in the initial conflict have sacrificed and set aside their differences in order to achieve a shared vision and common goal. When you fail to recognize the completion of a specific task and fail to celebrate these wins, the unintended message you send is that these tasks weren't really all that important to begin with.

Celebrating each task being completed solidifies the importance of resolving conflict, the importance of not allowing it to tear apart your organization, and the importance of working through it so as to build a stronger organization at the other end. Your people need to see you leading from the front, and if you don't celebrate the victories, neither will they. Inspiring and motivating your organization to learn the skillset needed to put aside their differences is a much simpler task to accomplish if they recognize that it is important enough to you that you celebrate it when it achieves your desired results.

It Doesn't Need to Break the Bank

Don't get wrapped up in throwing a huge party with catered finger foods and mimosas. You don't need a face painter, or a magic show, or even funnel cake. What your organization needs is you to openly and publicly recognize the importance of completing a task that directly correlated to your company's growth and success. Remember that monetary statistic from the opening pages? Teaching your organization how to effectively and efficiently resolve conflict keeps you from contributing to the $350B wasted annually on the negative effects of workplace conflict. If you really wanted to, you could spend that money celebrating your people instead of adding to the statistic.

Positive Conflict Starts Here

It should go without saying that celebrating the wins is an easy way to build an organizational culture where people are excited about going above and beyond what is expected of them in order to achieve more for the organization. The benefits are too numerous to list here, but you must know how important it is that you celebrate publicly and celebrate often. Encourage your people to follow your lead, and make sure you lead well. Take advantage of the savings you earn by teaching your organization to squash their differences and to work together, and ensure you celebrate right. Remember, once you get to this point in the process, you and your team have earned it.

CONCLUSION:

The Foundation

"Blood, sweat, and respect. The first two you give.

The last one you earn."

- Dwayne Johnson

You now have the foundation needed to effectively and efficiently resolve conflict within your workplace. My intent in writing this book was to demonstrate how simple this process truly is. As with anything in life, the more you do this, the easier it will become. Do not become discouraged through this process if you don't see the results you expect to see, or if this process takes longer than anticipated. Your focus needs to remain solely on doing what you can to get you and your team through as many of these keys as possible.

As a leader, you are responsible for the well-being of those you are charged to lead. This process is not easy. In fact, resolving conflict within the workplace is probably one of the most difficult tasks you will encounter as a leader. For this reason alone organizations throughout the nation waste more than $350B each year on the negative effects of conflict.

There is a huge difference between not knowing how to resolve conflict in your organization, and simply choosing to ignore it in the hopes it will go away on its own. The fact that you have read this book speaks to the type of leader you are. Don't shy away from the challenges because they're hard. Weak leaders shirk their responsibilities to those they lead, and poor leader abdicate their responsibilities to the organization they are supposed to be working for and improving. Don't allow yourself to shirk or abdicate your responsibilities when it comes to being a leader.

Jump into the mix, get your hands dirty, and help your organization create an organizational culture that stands together against conflict within the workplace. If the national statistic related to money wasted on the negative effects of conflict is to be reduced, it has to start with someone and it has to start somewhere. Why not let that someone be you, and why not let that somewhere be your organization?

ABOUT THE AUTHOR

 Dr. Stephen L. Kalaluhi is an organizational leadership expert, certified John Maxwell Team leadership speaker, trainer, and coach, adjunct professor, and founder of StephenK Leadership, a premier corporate leadership training and development company headquartered in San Diego, CA. Stephen believes that connecting an individual's purpose to their passion is how they truly make an impact in their world and become great as a leader. Stephen earned his Ph.D. in Organizational Leadership from Regent University's School of Business and Leadership. He currently resides in San Diego, CA with his beautiful wife of 22 years, and his two wonderful boys.

Email Stephen at:

Stephen@StephenKLeadership.com

Or Call Toll Free:

(844) YOU-LEAD

Made in the USA
San Bernardino, CA
13 February 2016